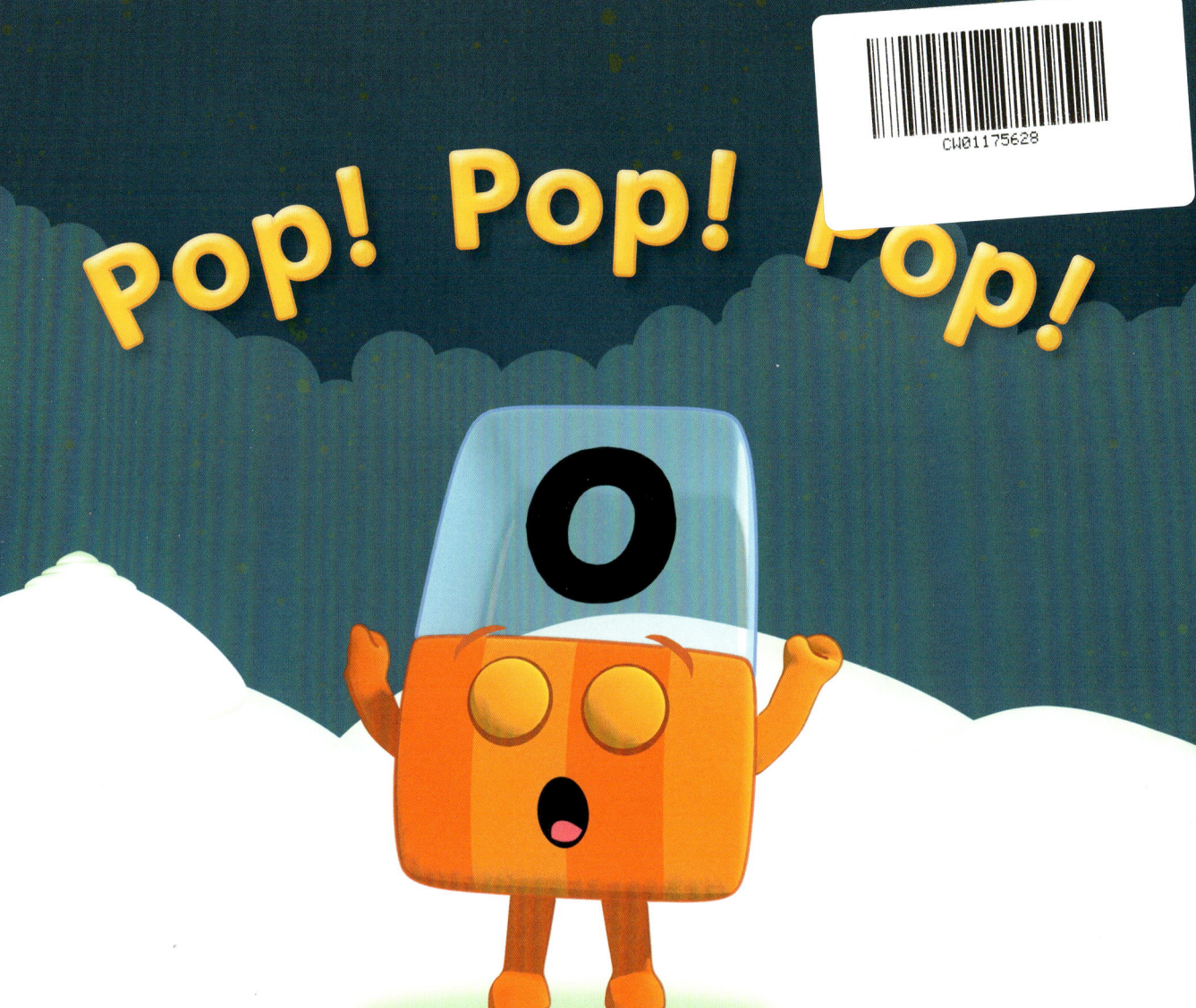

Pop! Pop! Pop!

Written by Joe Elliot
Illustrated by Neil Sutherland, Blue-Zoo and Tony Trimmer

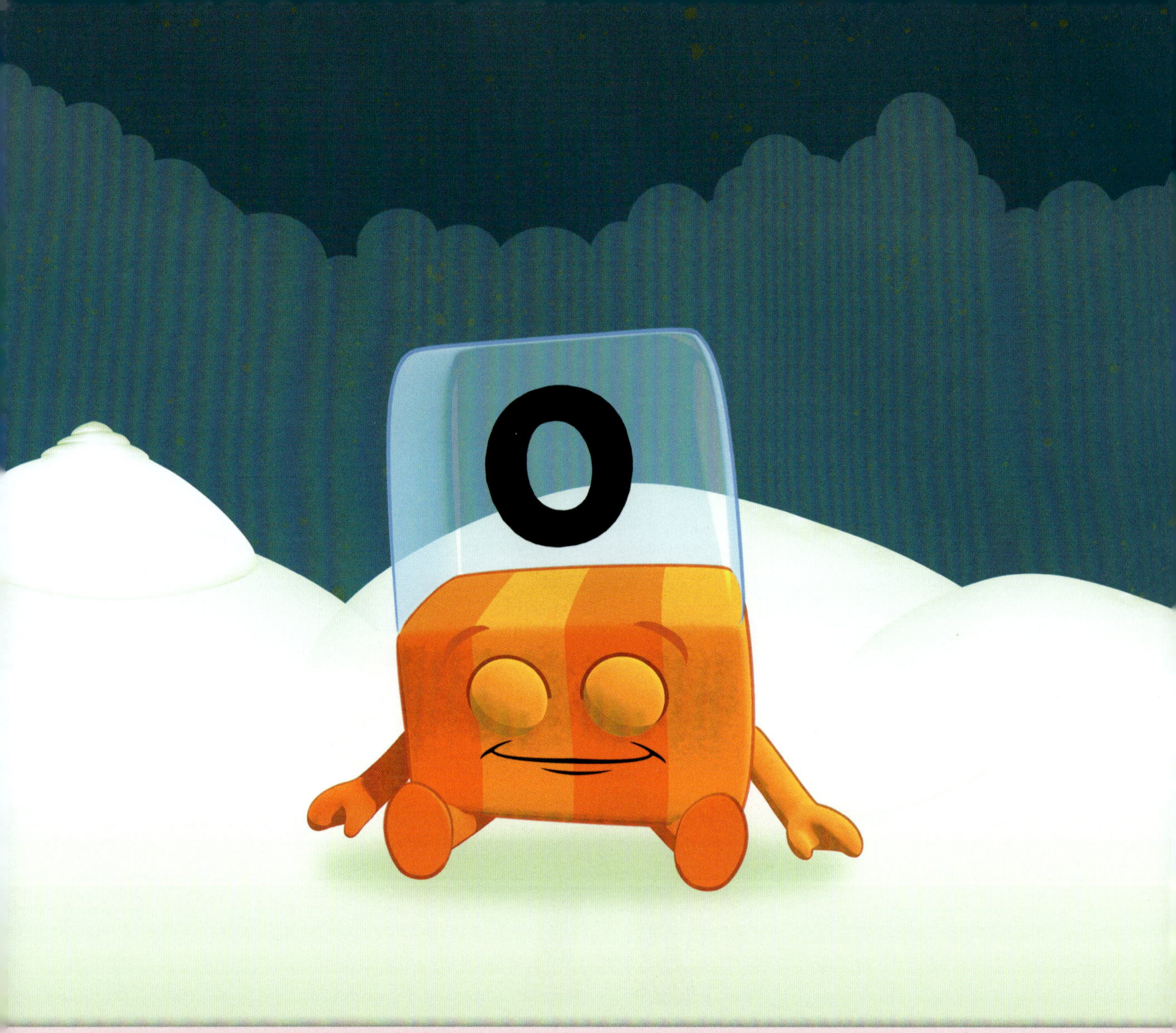

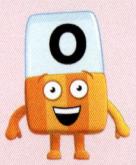 o nods.

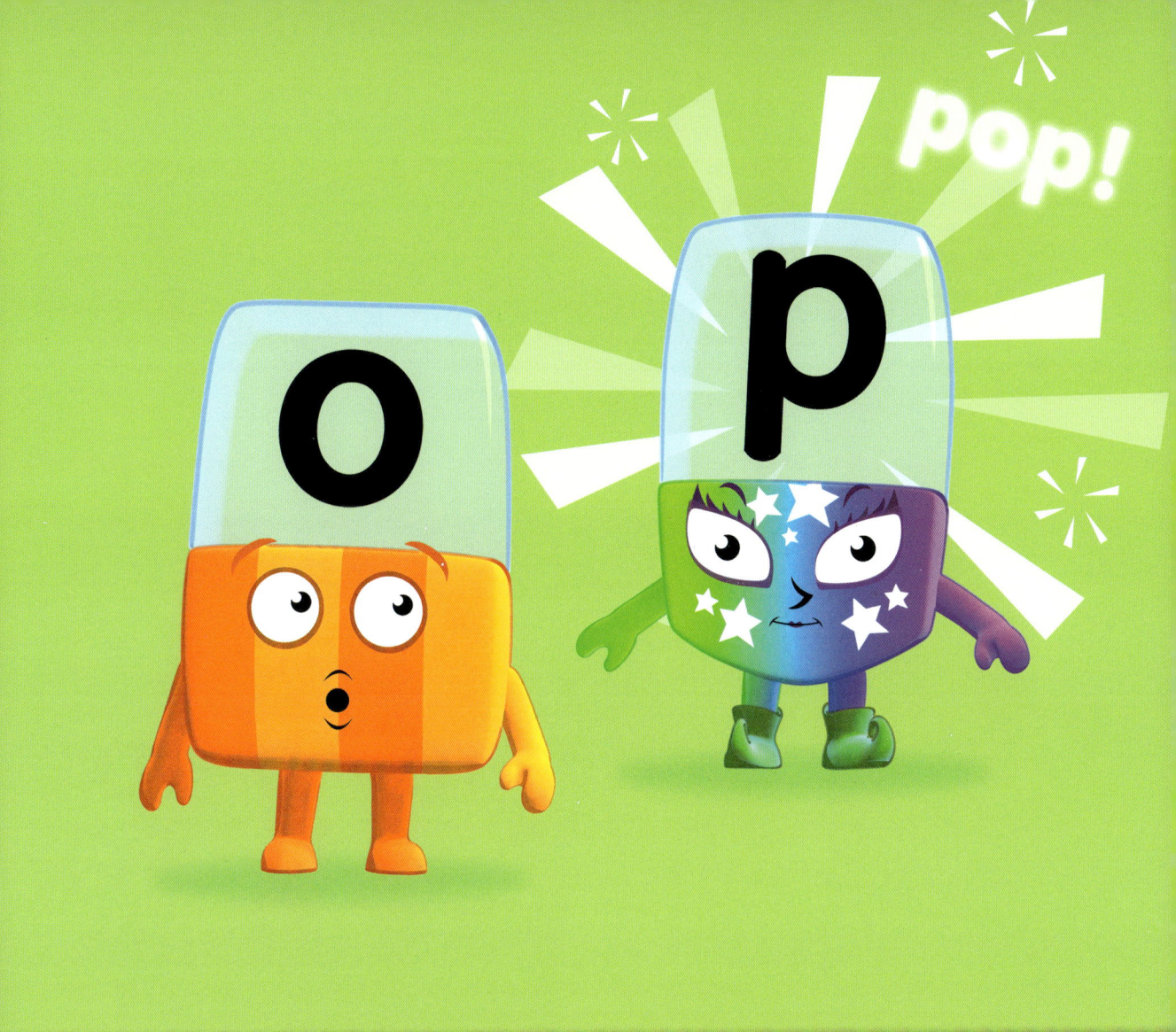

p pops in.

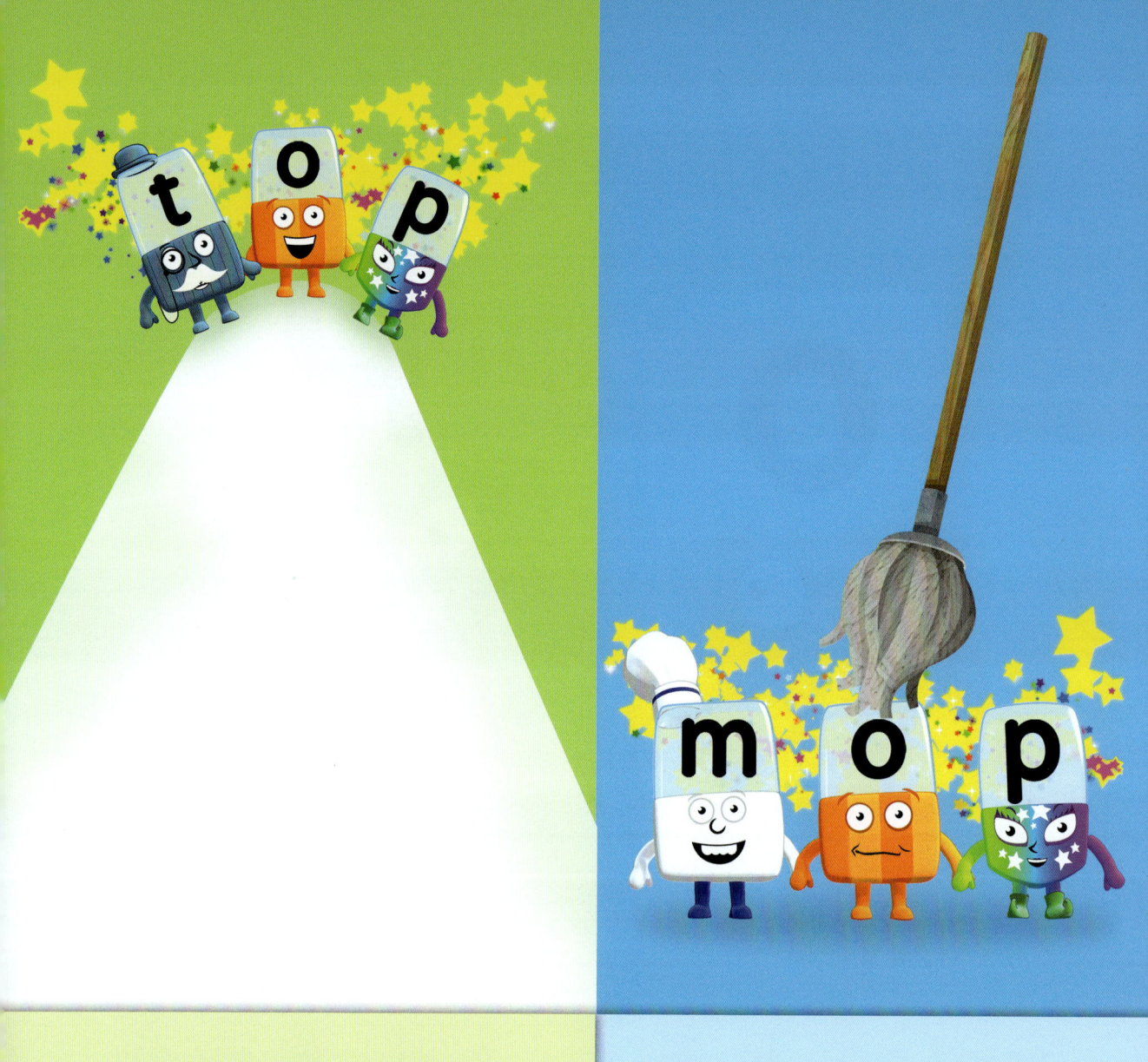

t-o-p, top!

m-o-p, mop!

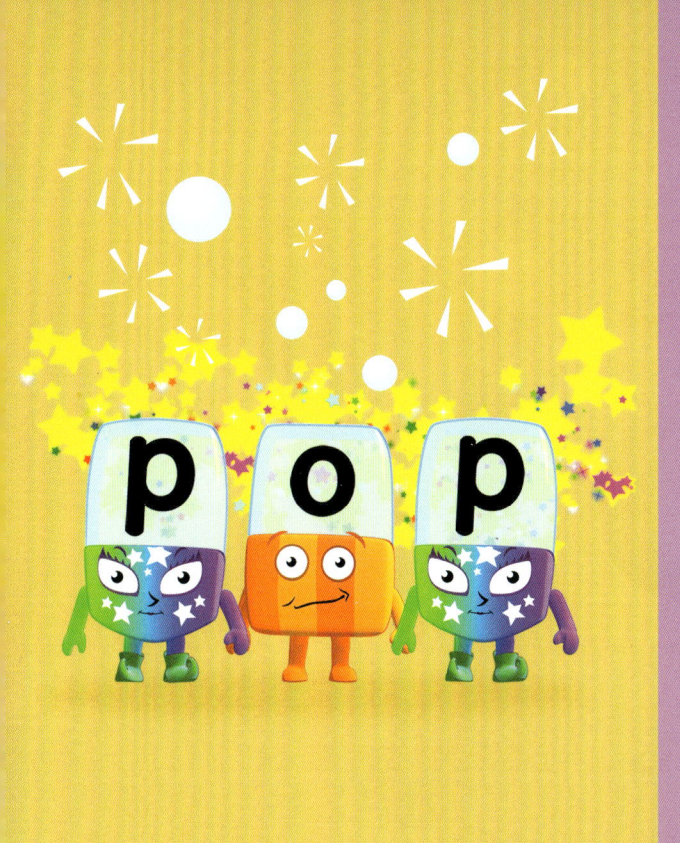

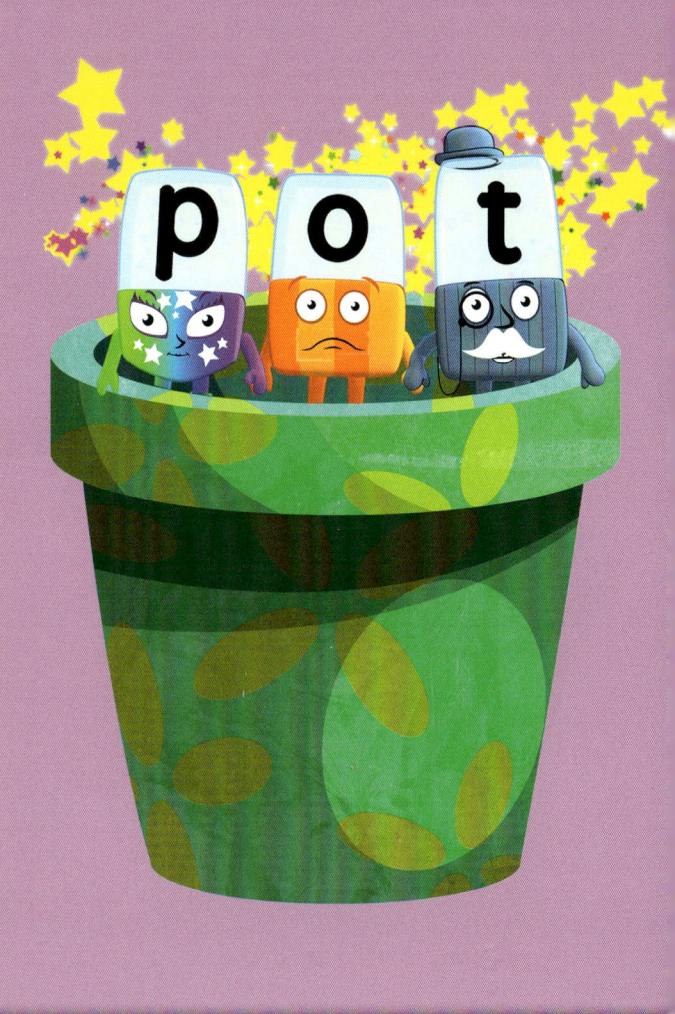

p-o-p, pop!

p-o-t, pot!

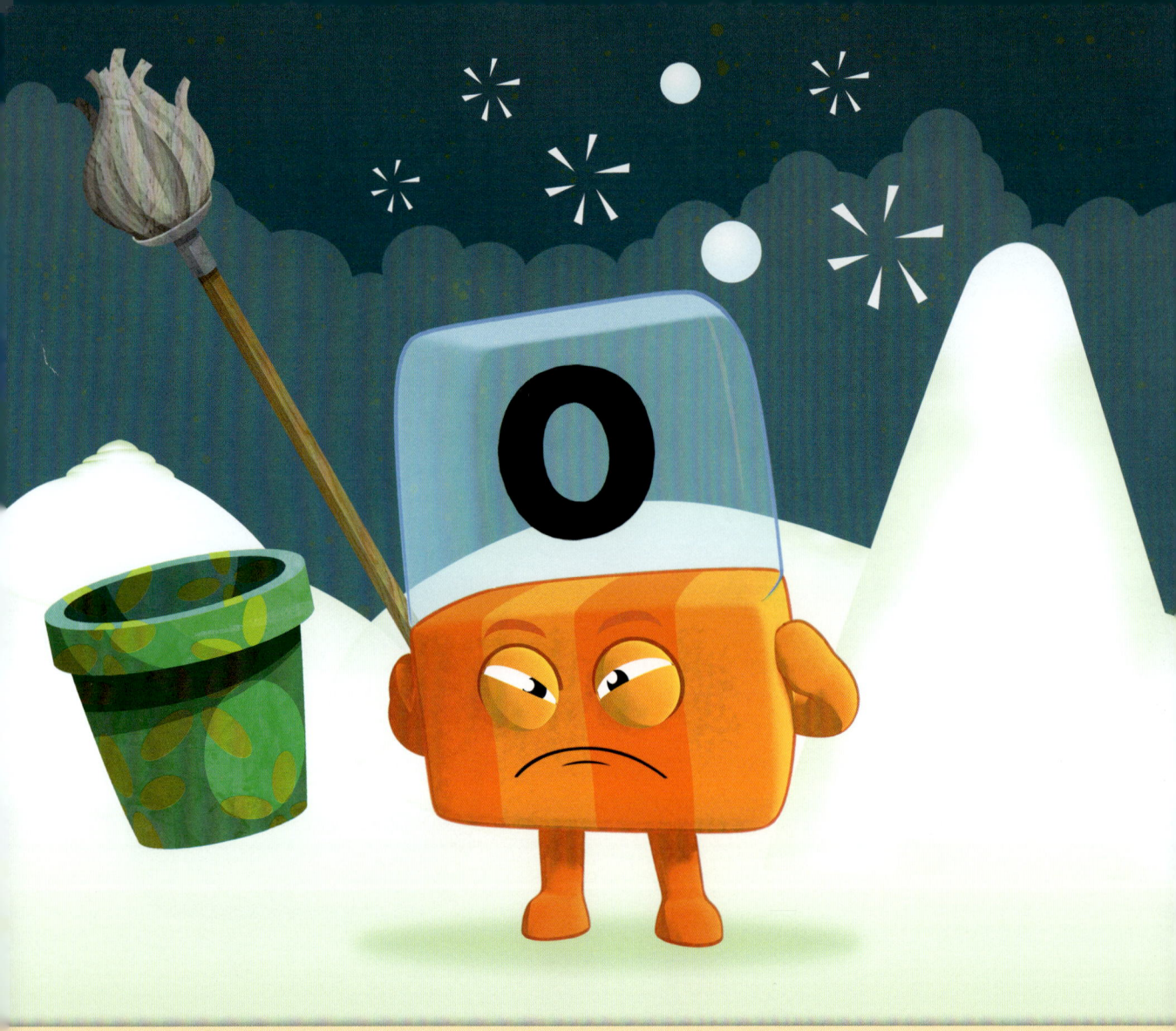

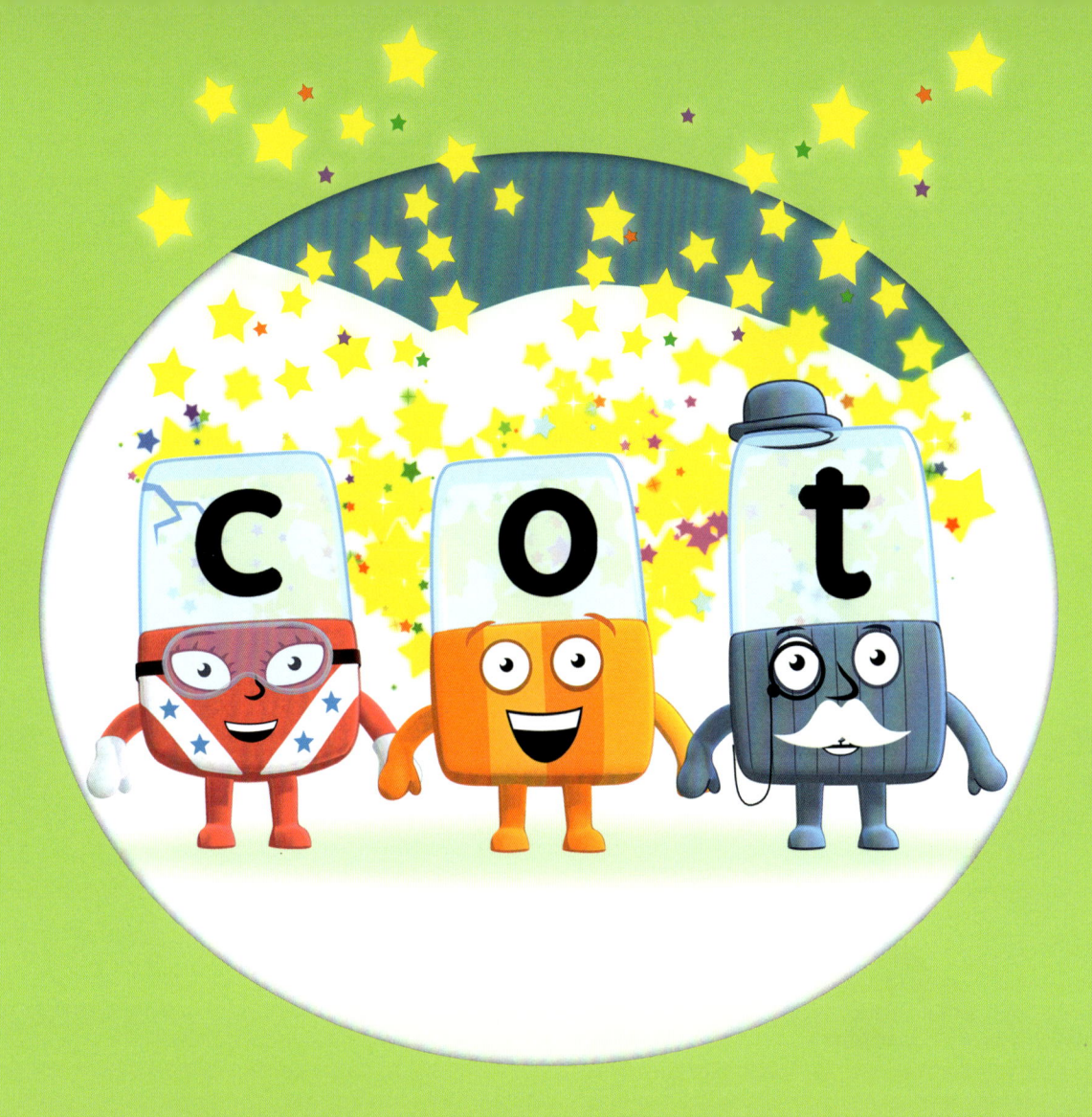

c-o-t, cot!

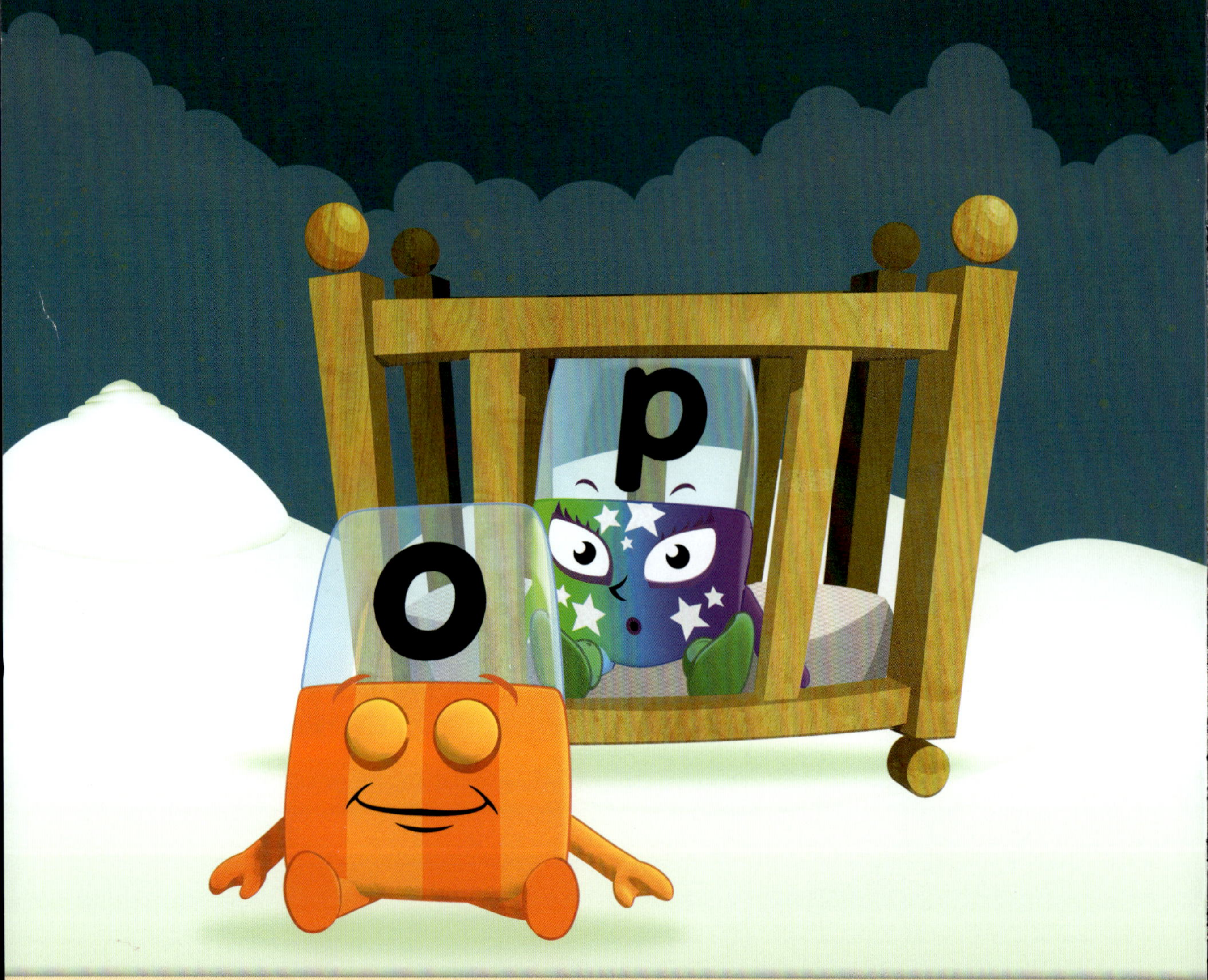

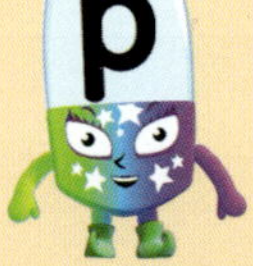

p pops in to a cot. 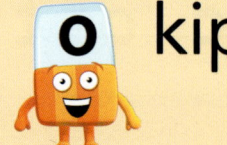 o kips.